RACING SPORTS

SUPERBIKE RACING

BY ANITA BANKS

WWW.APEXEDITIONS.COM

Apex is distributed by North Star Editions:
sales@northstareditions.com | 888-417-0195

Produced for Apex by Red Line Editorial.

Photographs ©: Pierre Stevenin/Cal Sport Media/ZUMA Wire/AP Images, cover; Shutterstock Images, 1, 4–5, 6–7, 8, 9, 10–11, 14, 16–17, 18–19, 20, 21, 22–23, 24–25, 26–27, 29; Guy Palmiotto/AP Images, 12; iStockphoto, 13

Library of Congress Control Number: 2023900132

ISBN
978-1-63738-540-1 (hardcover)
978-1-63738-594-4 (paperback)
978-1-63738-700-9 (ebook pdf)
978-1-63738-648-4 (hosted ebook)

Printed in the United States of America
Mankato, MN
082023

NOTE TO PARENTS AND EDUCATORS

Apex books are designed to build literacy skills in striving readers. Exciting, high-interest content attracts and holds readers' attention. The text is carefully leveled to allow students to achieve success quickly. Additional features, such as bolded glossary words for difficult terms, help build comprehension.

TABLE OF CONTENTS

CHAPTER 1

READY TO RACE

Superbike racers wait in their starting positions. The countdown begins. Then the green flag drops, and they speed off.

The best starting spot is called the pole position.

As the riders approach the first turn, they start **cornering**. They lean their bikes to one side. After the turn, they speed down the course.

Leaning helps riders go around the track's turns quickly.

FAST FACT

Some superbikes can go more than 200 miles per hour (322 km/h).

Most superbike races last around 40 minutes.

After several laps, the riders see a white flag. There is one lap left. One rider pulls ahead and crosses the finish line first.

TOP SPEED

If a bike speeds up too quickly, its front wheel can lift off the ground. That is called a wheelie. It slows the bike down. To go the fastest, riders keep their wheels just touching the ground.

Some riders do wheelies on purpose to celebrate after races.

CHAPTER 2

SUPERBIKE HISTORY

Superbike racing began in the United States in the 1970s. Companies had made motorcycles with powerful engines. People started to race them.

Honda began making the CB750 in 1969. It was the first motorcycle to be called a superbike.

Freddie Spencer was a popular racer in the 1980s. He raced Honda superbikes.

An early superbike race was held in 1973 at the Laguna Seca Raceway. It was very popular. So, the race happened again the next year.

FAST FACT

The first superbike **series** was AMA's Superbike Championship. It started in 1976.

Laguna Seca is a famous raceway. It has a difficult set of turns called the Corkscrew.

SHOEI
47
GA·BE SOLUTIONS
MOTOCORSA
CRETA
BORGO
epiù
PADANIA
Cereda Ambrogio
GENERALI
PIRELLI

Soon after, superbike racing became a new **class** of motorcycle racing. Groups formed to create the rules. Superbike racing spread to other countries. It became a global sport.

TV SPOTLIGHT

Cable TV helped superbike racing gain fans. At first, few races appeared on TV. But by the 1990s, channels like ESPN showed many races. They helped the sport become popular.

The Superbike World Championship has taken place each year since 1988.

CHAPTER 3

ABOUT THE RACES

Superbike races take place on paved courses. Each course has many curves. Racers complete several laps around it.

The TT Circuit Assen is a famous racing course in the Netherlands.

Racers compete in a series of races throughout the year. Each **round** in the series happens over one weekend. Riders get points based on their place in each race.

The top series of superbike racing in the United States is run by MotoAmerica.

FAST FACT

Most superbike courses are 2 to 4 miles (3.2 to 6.4 km) long.

Toprak Razgatlioglu won the World Superbike Championship in 2021.

At the end of the season, the rider with the most points is the champion. A series may also have a manufacturers' champion. That goes to the team with the fastest riders.

THE CREW

Each superbike racer works with a crew. A crew chief leads this group. This person is like a coach. The chief helps plan the best way to build and drive.

Mechanics help fix bikes before, during, and after races.

CHAPTER 4

EQUIPMENT

Superbikes start as regular road bikes. Companies like Ducati and Yamaha make them. Then, the bikes are **modified**.

Cubic centimeters (cc) is a way to measure engine size. Most superbikes have 750cc to 1200cc engines.

Each company makes changes to the bikes for their team. They might adjust the engines, brakes, and **suspensions**. They try to make the bikes as fast as possible.

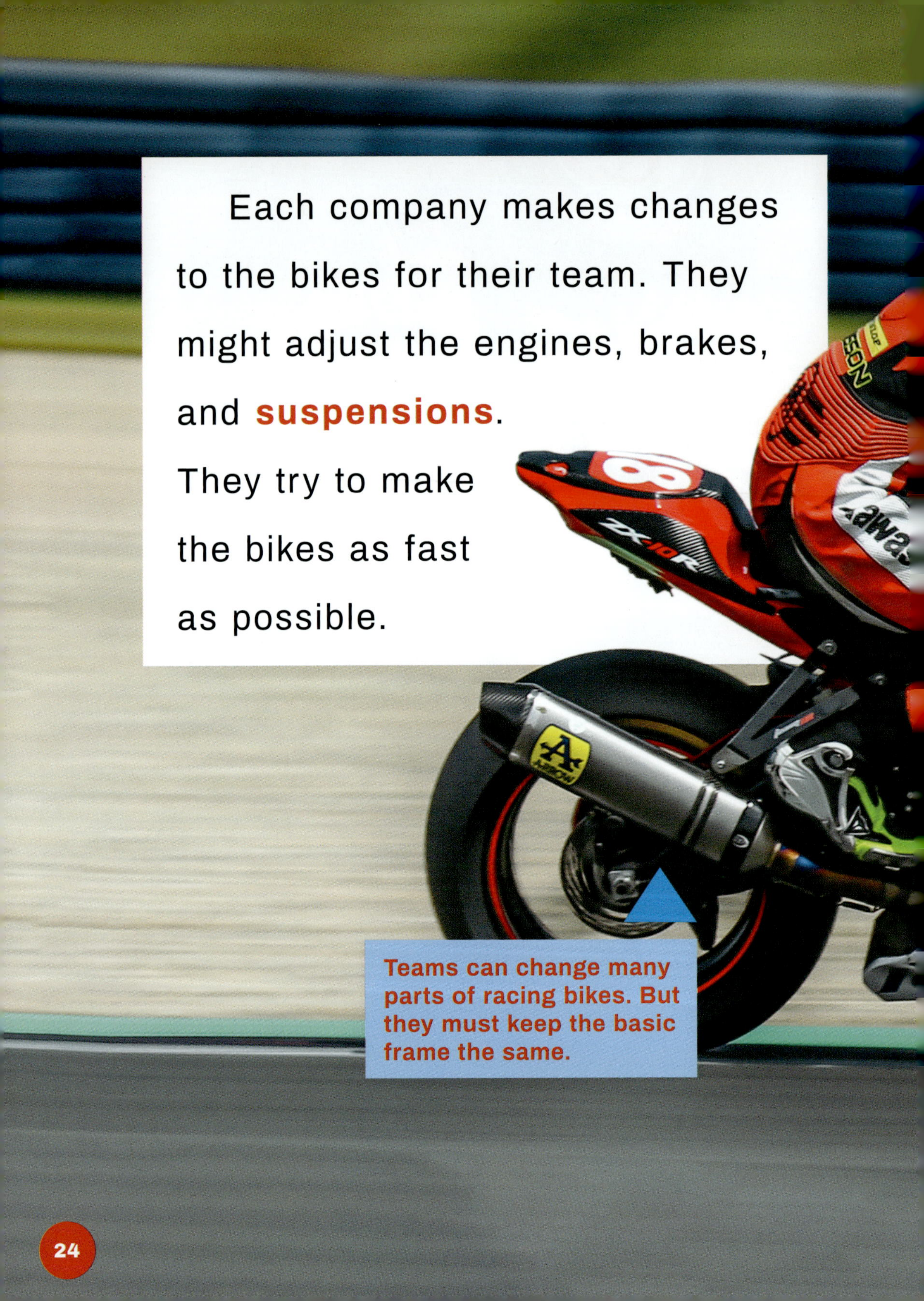

Teams can change many parts of racing bikes. But they must keep the basic frame the same.

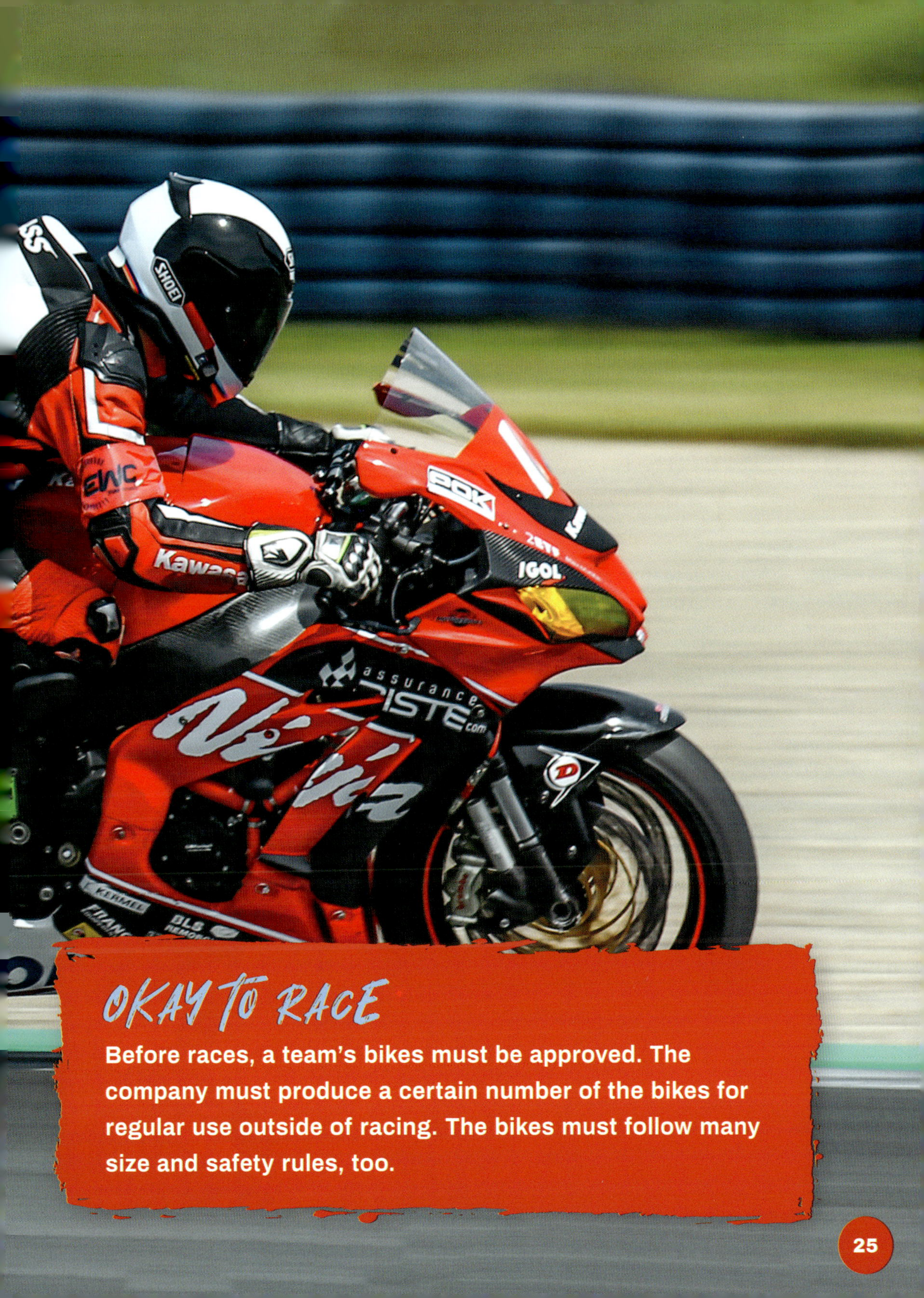

OKAY TO RACE

Before races, a team's bikes must be approved. The company must produce a certain number of the bikes for regular use outside of racing. The bikes must follow many size and safety rules, too.

Superbike racing can be dangerous. So, riders wear helmets and leather suits. These things protect riders if they crash.

FAST FACT

Some superbikes have airbags.

Kneepads help protect riders' legs as they lean during turns.

COMPREHENSION QUESTIONS

Write your answers on a separate piece of paper.

1. Write a few sentences that explain the main ideas of Chapter 2.
2. Would you want to try superbike racing? Why or why not?
3. Who is the manufacturers' champion?
   - **A.** the rider with the most points
   - **B.** the team with the fastest riders
   - **C.** a company that builds all the bikes
4. How could showing more races on TV help superbike racing gain fans?
   - **A.** People would stop watching races at tracks.
   - **B.** New viewers could find and watch races more easily.
   - **C.** People would be less likely to have favorite racers.

5. What does **global** mean in this book?

*Superbike racing spread to other countries. It became a **global** sport.*

A. happening around the world
B. happening in just one place
C. happening only in the past

6. What does **adjust** mean in this book?

*Each company makes changes to the bikes for their team. They might **adjust** the engines, brakes, and suspensions.*

A. stop using
B. keep the same
C. change

Answer key on page 32.

GLOSSARY

cable TV

A system that uses wires to send programs and channels to people's TVs.

class

A separate category of racing with its own rules.

cornering

Leaning the body and bike toward the ground during turns.

modified

Changed to be more suited to something.

round

One of several parts of a contest.

series

A set of superbike races that takes place each year.

suspensions

Systems on cars or bikes that protect people from feeling hard road or ground conditions.

TO LEARN MORE

BOOKS

Gagne, Tammy. *Cool Rides on Wheels: Electric Race Cars, Superbikes, and More*. North Mankato, MN: Capstone Press, 2021.

Hamilton, S. L. *The World's Fastest Motorcycles*. Minneapolis: Abdo Publishing, 2021.

Walker, Hubert. *World's Fastest Motorcycles*. Mendota Heights, MN: Apex Editions, 2022.

ONLINE RESOURCES

Visit **www.apexeditions.com** to find links and resources related to this title.

ABOUT THE AUTHOR

Anita Banks enjoys writing for children. She also enjoys reading, hiking, and traveling.

INDEX

ANSWER KEY:

1. Answers will vary; 2. Answers will vary; 3. B; 4. B; 5. A; 6. C